MEDITATE
don't
MEDICATE

A 14-Day Journey of
Letting Go and Finding Yourself

Aunna Pourang, MD

Cover photos by Lee Holt
Book design & layout by Summer R. Morris

Edited by Kimberly M. Smith
KMSmithWrites.com

Quotes from *Awareness,* copyright 1990, by the Center for Spiritual Exchange. Reprinted with permission.

DISCLAIMER
The information in this book is not intended or implied to be a substitute for professional medical advice, diagnosis, or treatment. All content is for general informational purposes only and does not guarantee particular results of any kind. The author does not assume any liability for the activities provided. While the title encourages meditation, it is important to note that medication is appropriate in certain circumstances when indicated by your healthcare provider. If you have any concerns regarding your health or a medical condition, you should promptly consult your healthcare provider.

For more information on health
and happiness visit www.draunna.com

Dedication

I dedicate this book to the Benevolent Universe and loving family and friends who have supported me on my own journey.

Contents

Mindful Self-Discovery

These days everything is fast paced. We can do almost anything without having to leave our houses. Everything is readily available—from smart phones to fast food. Yet with all the advanced technology available, we are growing unhealthier and increasingly stressed. We've traveled so far from health and happiness that we don't realize life is really meant to be enjoyed and lived to its fullest potential.

Many of us may feel as if we are out of touch with ourselves, as if something is "off" in our lives, and we cannot figure out what it could be. "It" feels uncomfortable. This feeling is related to avoiding what is going on inside of us rather than anything actually being wrong with us. So what do many of us do? We continue to avoid and become workaholics, blame others, or soothe feelings through unhealthy habits such as smoking, eating unhealthy food, and drinking alcohol. Many of us spend our entire lives avoiding, until we hit rock bottom and have no other choice but to change our lives around for the better.

A primary reason for dissatisfaction with anything in our lives comes from living unconsciously. Many of us just go through the motions of life. Often we don't question our habits or motives for anything. Some of these habits and motives for what we do in our lives can cause so much negativity. For example, take an unhealthy habit such as excessive eating, which can lead to obesity. If we struggle with this habit, we may look for every possible way to stop, with pills and diets, but often find ourselves back where we started. We may not question the underlying reason for

1

why we overeat. Living consciously may reveal that the reason is to calm our anxiety or because we learned the habit as children. When we can bring the deeper root causes of our issues to light, we can make effective and healthy changes.

Another cause for discontent in our lives comes from a lack of self-appreciation. When we appreciate ourselves, we know our true worth. We treat our bodies as the temple that houses our soul, a soul that came to this earth to contribute beautiful things to the Universe and to experience the beauty of life. When we know our worth, we feed our bodies healthy foods and keep our bodies active with exercise. We find time to sleep and release stress. The question becomes why we don't know or feel this core inherent value. If we take the time to examine our self-talk or thoughts, we may find there is a lot of negativity present. This negativity often comes from something someone said to us or did to us in our distant past to make us feel as if we were not good enough. If we continue to live unconsciously, we perpetuate this negativity in our present lives and from generation to generation. We can stop this cycle by living consciously. So how do we live consciously? By being in the present moment at all times. By consistently being aware of all underlying thoughts, habits, emotions, and bodily sensations. This is what mindfulness is all about.

The purpose of this guidebook is to start a journey of finding yourself, to find some of the reasons you unconsciously prevent yourself from living a healthy and happy life, and to make the conscious decisions that enable you to start living a fulfilling life. This journey is not limited, however, to fourteen days. It is an experience that takes place at every moment for the rest of your life. This program is to help open the doors to that path.

If you are searching for more meaning in life, whether it's a better job, health, or happiness, chances are you've been looking in the wrong places. It all starts with you. Let's find that beautiful and valuable you that has always existed and always will.

Tips for Your 14-Day Journey

This guide is designed to be completed over a period of two weeks. Each day I provide different exercises in the forms of reflection, activities, and reading. A daily log sheet allows you to record your food and liquid intake, sleep, and physical and stress release activities. This log helps you be mindful of your daily habits. It is optional as to whether or not you want to calculate your calories or measure your steps. Many great mobile device calorie-counting applications, as well as pedometers and activity trackers, are available on the market.

I've also included a daily gratitude log. Every day before bed, write down what you are grateful for, even if it's something as simple as having the shirt on your back. There is also room available for daily affirmations and miscellaneous reflection. I recommend that you keep a separate journal for additional reflection.

JOURNALING TIPS:

Be Patient and Keep it Simple

As exciting as it is to begin making positive changes in your life, I encourage you to complete this guide in no sooner than two weeks. You'll find that you'll be discovering many aspects of yourself and may even have some emotions arise. It's important not to overwhelm yourself. You may even need to take a break and come back another day. This journey is meant to be enjoyable, so remember to keep it simple.

The Only Way Out is Through

The journey of finding yourself is not always the easiest task. When facing ourselves, our past, and our bad habits to get to the roots of our issues, we may find that some painful emotions we have not dealt with come up. Often it is this pain that we avoid. You have the amazing courage to transform your life, and once you get through the pain, you can let it go forever.

Honesty

During the reflections throughout the guidebook, I encourage you to be completely honest with yourself. This is a time for you to get to know yourself in a judgment-free environment, whether it is judgment from yourself or others around you. You are worthy of a happy life, and no one else has a right to take that from you.

Limit Exposure to Technology

Often, the distractions of daily life are what prevent us from getting in touch with ourselves. Consider limiting your exposure to technology on a daily basis for the next fourteen days. Only use your cell phone when necessary. Limit your time for e-mails and social media to less than an hour per day. Use the time you would normally watch TV for performing the activities provided.

You are worthy of a
happy and healthy life.

Day 1:
Reflect and Affirm

1. Look into a mirror and say the following: "I love you, you are amazing!"

2. How did this feel?

_____

_____

_____

_____

_____

_____

_____

_____

_____

3. If it feels strange or you do not believe it, then ask yourself why? Reflect on it below.

_____

_____

_____

_____

_____

_____

_____

_____

_____

_____

Many of us have adopted a negative view of ourselves. Our thoughts and self-talk are also frequently negative. We may not realize this because it has become second nature. Deep down, everyone really is amazing. It is not about accomplishments, money, or fame; our inherent value comes from the fact that we are human and imperfect, and this is what makes us perfect! We are all born with inherent worth, but somewhere in our past, circumstances such as abuse, relationships, or hurtful words and actions have caused us to have a negative image of ourselves. Unfortunately, these images and negative words become ones that we accept about ourselves. The good news is this can change with mindfulness. When we become aware of the negative things we say or think about ourselves, we can replace them at that moment with positive statements. A great way to do this is with positive affirmations. Affirmations are declarations. Our subconscious mind will accept whatever affirmations it receives. If it receives negative affirmations, such as negative thoughts about ourselves, we will perpetuate negativity in our lives. So why not affirm positivity?

4. For the next activity, think of someone for whom you care. Write a list of things you like about them in the following way: "You are wonderful."/"You are beautiful."

_____

_____

_____

_____

_____

_____

_____

_____

_____

5. For everything you wrote above, cross out "You" and replace it with "I." Then tell yourself these things aloud.

_____

_____

_____

_____

_____

_____

_____

_____

_____

6. Write a list of your own affirmations.

_____

_____

_____

_____

_____

_____

_____

_____

After writing your affirmations, repeat them every day. There will be some additional affirmations provided throughout the guide.

TIPS FOR AFFIRMATIONS:

- Affirmations can be written about anything. For example, if you are overweight and would like to be fit, a great affirmation to state would be, "I am healthy and fit." While on a physical level you may not feel fit, your subconscious mind will eventually adopt a healthy mindset and bring about changes to fulfill the affirmation.

- It is important to state affirmations in the present tense and not in future tense. Again, the subconscious mind needs specific instructions. Instead of saying, "I will be successful," which is always in the future, say, "I am successful."

- It's important to give the subconscious mind positive thoughts at all times. Avoid using negative words such as "not," "never," "nothing," or "no," etc. For example, instead of saying, "I am not disorganized," say, "I am organized."

- The more you say and practice positive affirmations, the more your subconscious mind will accept them.

- *Believe* and visualize yourself achieving your goals! Really make an effort to feel it. Your subconscious mind will process affirmations with belief and faith. Even if you do not fully accept the content of the positive affirmation, try your best to believe. It may seem strange at first but keep doing it and see the wonderful things that will start to happen in your life.

DAILY LOG: Day 1

NUTRITION LOG

Today I ate

Breakfast _____

Lunch _____

Dinner _____

Snacks _____

Drinks _____

Total calories consumed _____

Cravings _____

Total amount of water consumed _____

SLEEP LOG

Yesterday I slept _____ hours.

ACTIVITY LOG

Today I took _____ steps.

Types of physical activities performed _____

_____

_____

_____

_____

STRESS RELEASE LOG

Today I released stress by _____

_____

_____

_____

_____

GRATITUDE LOG

Today I am grateful for _____

_____

_____

_____

_____

MISCELLANEOUS REFLECTION

_____

_____

_____

_____

_____

_____

_____

_____

_____

Today remember,
it's about the journey,
not the destination.

Day 2:
Intention

I set positive goals in my life and achieve them to my fullest potential.

1. What are your goals in life?

---

2. What do you hope to achieve from this book? Examples: More happiness, get to know myself better, etc.

_____

_____

_____

_____

_____

_____

_____

_____

3. Setting intentions are like building a foundation for your life. Getting clear on your goals will help you develop the plans necessary to achieve them. Write your goals in the form of an affirmation and practice them every day. For example, if you want more happiness, state, "I am full of happiness at all times," or simply, "I am happy!"

_____

_____

_____

_____

_____

_____

_____

_____

4. For each thing you wrote in number two, ask yourself why you want it. Continue to ask yourself why until you cannot answer the question anymore. Example: I want to lose weight. Why? Because I want to look good. Why? Because I do not feel attractive. Why? . . . and so forth.

_____

_____

_____

_____

_____

_____

_____

_____

5. Review what you have written in the above question. Are there any common themes?

_____

_____

_____

_____

_____

_____

_____

_____

6. Often our motives for wanting certain things are completely different than the actual things we want. The deeper reason may actually relate to wanting to be happy, secure, accepted, or some other reason(s) unique to you. Take some time to reflect on this below.

_____

_____

_____

_____

_____

_____

_____

DAILY LOG: Day 2

NUTRITION LOG

Today I ate

Breakfast _____

Lunch _____

Dinner _____

Snacks _____

Drinks _____

Total calories consumed _____

Cravings _____

Total amount of water consumed _____

SLEEP LOG

Yesterday I slept _____ hours.

ACTIVITY LOG

Today I took _____ steps.

Types of physical activities performed _____

_____

_____

_____

_____

STRESS RELEASE LOG

Today I released stress by _____

_____

_____

_____

_____

GRATITUDE LOG

Today I am grateful for _____

_____

_____

_____

_____

MISCELLANEOUS REFLECTION

_____

_____

_____

_____

_____

_____

_____

_____

_____

_____

Today smile at someone
you have never met.

Day 3:
Life's Mirror

Affirmation

Life reflects back to me the beauty that lies within.

1. Examine your life and surroundings. What do you wish could be different?

_____

_____

_____

_____

_____

_____

_____

_____

2. When things in our lives are not as we would like them to be, it's easy to blame external circumstances. The key to changing what is happening outside of us is by changing what is happening within us. List the answers from question one in column one. Then in column two, list what inside of you could be the cause. Some examples are listed below.

1. Things I don't want or like	2. Reason it is in my life
Unhealthy relationship	*Poor relationship with self*
Struggles with money	*Negative mindset toward abundance*
Cluttered house	*Cluttered mind*
Irritated about someone else's insecurities	*Not addressing my own insecurities*

1. Things I don't want or like	2. Reason it is in my life

Our external world reflects what is happening internally. Working on what is inside of us will bring what we want on the outside. Obviously, certain things outside of us are beyond our control, but we have the option to find a solution or to react to it in a more positive way. Therefore, the next time something isn't going the way you want around you, don't react negatively or blame. Take a step back, look within, and you will find a solution.

NUTRITION LOG

Today I ate

Breakfast _____

Lunch _____

Dinner _____

Snacks _____

Drinks _____

Total calories consumed _____

Cravings _____

Total amount of water consumed _____

SLEEP LOG

Yesterday I slept _____ hours.

ACTIVITY LOG

Today I took _____ steps.

Types of physical activities performed _____

_____

_____

_____

_____

STRESS RELEASE LOG

Today I released stress by _____

_____

_____

_____

_____

GRATITUDE LOG

Today I am grateful for _____

_____

_____

_____

_____

MISCELLANEOUS REFLECTION

_____

_____

_____

_____

_____

_____

_____

_____

_____

_____

Today embrace that your perfection lies in the fact that you are imperfect.

Day 4:
Acceptance

Affirmation

I accept where I am in life and know that life always has wonderful things to offer me.

1. Were there any goals during your reflection on Day 2 that you have had difficulty achieving in the past? If so, why? Examples: procrastination, fear, etc.

_____

_____

_____

_____

_____

_____

_____

2. During Day 2 of the journey, we examined deeper underlying motives for what we actually want. What are some reasons you have been unable to sustain happiness, security, acceptance, or other mental or emotional states? Examples: low self-esteem, issues from the past, etc.

_____

_____

_____

_____

_____

_____

_____

During any time of reflection, we tend to look at all the "mistakes" we have made. This process brings up many different emotions, such as feeling inadequate or regretful of our past actions. This reaction is natural. If we did not have these feelings, we would not think about making any changes. It's crucial to allow ourselves to feel the emotions but not to be stuck dwelling in regret only to become angry or depressed. Resisting our current situation takes away precious energy and clarity to make positive changes and find solutions. Today accept where you are and everything as it is, even if it's not what you want. Instead focus on the present moment and allow life to bring you the solutions you seek.

DAILY LOG: Day 4

NUTRITION LOG

Today I ate

Breakfast _____

Lunch _____

Dinner _____

Snacks _____

Drinks _____

Total calories consumed _____

Cravings _____

Total amount of water consumed _____

SLEEP LOG

Yesterday I slept _____ hours.

ACTIVITY LOG

Today I took _____ steps.

Types of physical activities performed _____

_____

_____

_____

_____

STRESS RELEASE LOG

Today I released stress by _____

_____

_____

_____

_____

GRATITUDE LOG

Today I am grateful for _____

_____

_____

_____

_____

MISCELLANEOUS REFLECTION

_____

_____

_____

_____

_____

_____

_____

_____

_____

Today any time you have a
negative thought, immediately
think of something positive.

Day 5:
Forgiveness

Affirmation

*I forgive everyone who has contributed negativity to my life,
including myself.*

1. List anyone you have anger toward or are holding a grudge
   against. Is there anyone in your life who needs your forgiveness
   for something?

_____

_____

_____

_____

_____

_____

_____

_____

2. Is there anything you would like to forgive yourself about? Maybe you intentionally or unintentionally hurt someone else. Maybe you are upset with yourself for not taking care of your health.

_____

_____

_____

_____

_____

_____

_____

_____

3. On a subconscious level, we often hold ourselves accountable for the harmful actions of others, such as in the cases of abuse or dysfunctional relationships. This deep regret can cause emotional suffering. Self-forgiveness can heal this. Reflect on what you think about this truth.

_____

_____

_____

_____

_____

_____

_____

_____

_____

4. Using information from the previous answers, create your own forgiveness statements and then read them aloud. Examples: <u>Name of person</u> I forgive you for what you have done to me; I forgive myself for any mistakes I have made.

_____

_____

_____

_____

_____

_____

_____

_____

Eleanor Roosevelt once said, "No one can make you feel inferior without your consent." While it is true that some people may intentionally want to hurt us, most of the time people do not mean to hurt us. Hurt people hurt people. No one who feels whole inside has the need to hurt anyone else. Just as much as we have the ability to give our power to others by blaming them, we also have the power to forgive and let go. Forgiveness does not necessarily mean keeping those people in our lives, rather letting go of the mental and emotional associations we have attached to that person(s). Often we think we are punishing the other person by not forgiving them, but in actuality, we punish ourselves with the negative energy and emotions we hold in our body. Eleanor Roosevelt's words extend to ourselves as well. Energy is valuable, and forgiveness and letting go of negativity allows more positivity into our lives.

DAILY LOG: Day 5

NUTRITION LOG

Today I ate

Breakfast _____

Lunch _____

Dinner _____

Snacks _____

Drinks _____

Total calories consumed _____

Cravings _____

Total amount of water consumed _____

SLEEP LOG

Yesterday I slept _____ hours.

ACTIVITY LOG

Today I took _____ steps.

Types of physical activities performed _____

_____

_____

_____

_____

STRESS RELEASE LOG

Today I released stress by _____

_____

_____

_____

_____

GRATITUDE LOG

Today I am grateful for _____

_____

_____

_____

_____

MISCELLANEOUS REFLECTION

_____

_____

_____

_____

_____

_____

_____

_____

_____

Today pick a bad habit and
give it up for the day.

Day 6:
Control

Affirmation

I am a cocreator with the Universe in manifesting a wonderful life.

1. Over what aspects of your life do you feel you have control?

_____

_____

_____

_____

_____

_____

_____

2. In what aspects of your life do you feel powerless?

_____

_____

_____

_____

_____

_____

_____

_____

3. Is there anything that you try hard to control? If so, in what ways do you do this and why?

_____

_____

_____

_____

_____

_____

_____

4. Some additional things to reflect on:

    a. Has control, logic, worry, fear, or analysis brought you what you seek to control?

b. What is under the surface of what you are trying to control?

c. Could it be that the things you try to control, you actually have no control over?

d. While we do not have complete control over all circumstances, in what ways do you have control in certain situations?

e. What would happen if you were to let go of control?

_____

_____

_____

_____

_____

_____

_____

_____

_____

_____

_____

_____

_____

Day 6: Control

_____

_____

_____

_____

_____

_____

_____

_____

_____

_____

_____

_____

_____

_____

_____

_____

DAILY LOG: Day 6

NUTRITION LOG
Today I ate

Breakfast _____

Lunch _____

Dinner _____

Snacks _____

Drinks _____

Total calories consumed _____

Cravings _____

Total amount of water consumed _____

SLEEP LOG

Yesterday I slept _____ hours.

ACTIVITY LOG

Today I took _____ steps.

Types of physical activities performed _____

_____

_____

_____

_____

STRESS RELEASE LOG

Today I released stress by _____

_____

_____

_____

_____

GRATITUDE LOG

Today I am grateful for _____

_____

_____

_____

_____

MISCELLANEOUS REFLECTION

_____

_____

_____

_____

_____

_____

_____

_____

_____

Today practice relaxation.

If you feel pressure from yourself,
monitor your self-talk. Let go of feeling
that you have to/need to/should do something.
Take a break and then allow yourself to do
what you can in that moment.

Day 7:
Organization

Affirmation

Everything in my life is in perfect balance.

Activity:

Is clutter in your house in need of clearing? Perhaps you've saved old boxes of clothes or piles of papers. Today take an hour to eliminate some of that clutter. Recycle old papers you do not need. Donate any old clothes you have not worn in years. Maybe it's time to rid yourself of your ex's belongings. It's important to keep life as simple as you can. It doesn't help your life if things get in the way. If you have not needed to use something for the past two years, it's just taking up valuable space in your home. If you're having difficulty deciding to let go of certain things, put them in a box and return to this box six months later. If you have not needed the contents for any reason, this is a good sign it's time to release them. Even though this is an exercise dedicated to this day of the program, take time each week to rid yourself of more things you do not need.

1. Give yourself a few moments to reflect on why you may have been holding onto certain things.

_____

_____

_____

_____

_____

_____

_____

_____

2. What does holding onto these things contribute to your life, besides additional clutter?

_____

_____

_____

_____

_____

_____

3. What do you think will happen if you let go of these things?

_____

_____

_____

_____

_____

_____

_____

4.   Is there anything you are holding onto mentally or emotionally? (Usually this is something that is the hardest to let go.)

_____

_____

_____

_____

_____

_____

We also may experience disappointment when we are attached to certain outcomes that don't go the way we want. Usually something deeper lies under the surface of the things, people, emotions, or memories to which we cling. It could be that these things provide a sense of security or comfort, or that letting go of them signifies something negative. The reason will be unique to you. When we hold onto anything in life, however, we prevent new and positive experiences from coming in. This is not to say that it is not OK to experience emotions or save certain items of sentimental value. It's also OK to have goals and expectations. It is through loving detachment and getting in the habit of letting go at every moment that we keep life simple and lively.

DAILY LOG: Day 7

NUTRITION LOG

Today I ate

Breakfast _____

Lunch _____

Dinner _____

Snacks _____

Drinks _____

Total calories consumed _____

Cravings _____

Total amount of water consumed _____

SLEEP LOG

Yesterday I slept _____ hours.

ACTIVITY LOG

Today I took _____ steps.

Types of physical activities performed _____

_____

_____

_____

_____

STRESS RELEASE LOG

Today I released stress by _____

_____

_____

_____

_____

GRATITUDE LOG

Today I am grateful for _____

_____

_____

_____

_____

MISCELLANEOUS REFLECTION

_____

_____

_____

_____

_____

_____

_____

_____

_____

Today donate your time or money to a charitable cause.

Day 8:
Letting Go

Affirmation

*I release what no longer serves my highest good and allow the
abundance of life to flow to me.*

1. On the next page, in the present tense, write down everything of
   which you want to let go. Example: I release negativity in my life;
   I let go of unhealthy habits.

2. Repeat the statements you wrote on the next page aloud. Then
   remove the sheet from the book and take it to a place where
   you can safely burn it over a piece of cardboard or newspaper so
   that you can collect the ashes. (Please take extreme caution when
   using fire and make sure to read the disclaimer at the beginning
   of the guidebook. You may also rip up the paper and throw it
   away instead.) Take the ashes to a body of water such as a beach
   or a lake. If you do not have access to these settings, wash the
   ashes down the sink or a drain. These things are now a part of
   your past. Take a deep breath and acknowledge that you have let
   go of them forever.

Activity:

THINGS I WANT TO LET GO

_____

_____

_____

_____

_____

_____

_____

_____

_____

_____

_____

_____

_____

_____

_____

_____

_____

_____

_____

Day 8: Letting Go

_____

_____

_____

_____

_____

_____

_____

_____

_____

_____

_____

_____

_____

_____

_____

_____

_____

_____

_____

_____

_____

3. After performing the activity, reflect on the experience.

_____

_____

_____

_____

_____

_____

_____

_____

_____

_____

During the past few days, you may have focused on things you want or don't have, or even things you do not want in your life anymore. You may have learned some new and deeper things about yourself. Anthony de Mello once said, "Psychological insight is a great help, not analysis, however; analysis is paralysis. Insight is not necessarily analysis." While being mindful of the underlying motives and reasons for what we do and how we feel is important, it's also important not to be caught up in analyzing. Just like resisting and not accepting our current situation can prevent us from making positive changes, so can overanalyzing. So after understanding and accepting, remember to let go.

DAILY LOG: Day 8

NUTRITION LOG

Today I ate

Breakfast _____

Lunch _____

Dinner _____

Snacks _____

Drinks _____

Total calories consumed _____

Cravings _____

Total amount of water consumed _____

SLEEP LOG

Yesterday I slept _____ hours.

ACTIVITY LOG

Today I took _____ steps.

Types of physical activities performed _____

_____

_____

_____

_____

STRESS RELEASE LOG

Today I released stress by _____

_____

_____

_____

_____

GRATITUDE LOG

Today I am grateful for _____

_____

_____

_____

_____

MISCELLANEOUS REFLECTION

_____

_____

_____

_____

_____

_____

_____

_____

_____

_____

Day 1: Reflect And Affirm

_____

_____

_____

_____

_____

_____

_____

_____

_____

_____

_____

_____

_____

_____

_____

_____

_____

_____

_____

_____

_____

_____

Today try to see the good in everyone, even those for whom you do not necessarily care.

Day 9:
Faith

Affirmation

I have faith that everything in my life is working out perfectly.

1. Earlier you wrote a list of things you want in your life. From that list, write down anything that you have believed you could not attain or achieve.

_____

_____

_____

_____

_____

_____

_____

_____

2. Now write about what this belief of not being able to attain or achieve what you want in life has created.

_____

_____

_____

_____

_____

_____

_____

_____

_____

_____

_____

Our beliefs are self-fulfilling prophecies. Many times we lack faith in a higher power or ourselves. This lack of faith may be a result of the lack of faith our early caregivers had in themselves or in us. Likewise, it may be due to the fact that we have not realized how amazing we are just for being who we are. Regardless of your religious beliefs, faith is quite powerful. When we believe positive things can and are coming our way, with patience we allow life to work with us and for us. So even when everything seems like it has hit rock bottom, keep the faith. Look at where the lack of faith has gotten you.

DAILY LOG: Day 9

NUTRITION LOG

Today I ate

Breakfast _____

Lunch _____

Dinner _____

Snacks _____

Drinks _____

Total calories consumed _____

Cravings _____

Total amount of water consumed _____

SLEEP LOG

Yesterday I slept _____ hours.

ACTIVITY LOG

Today I took _____ steps.

Types of physical activities performed _____

_____

_____

_____

_____

STRESS RELEASE LOG

Today I released stress by _____

_____

_____

_____

_____

GRATITUDE LOG

Today I am grateful for _____

_____

_____

_____

_____

MISCELLANEOUS REFLECTION

_____

_____

_____

_____

_____

_____

_____

_____

_____

Today try something new.

Day 10:
Mindfulness Meditation

Affirmation
I am aware of the inner peace accessible to me at every moment.

Activity:

This book provides different mindfulness techniques, including reflection, awareness, appreciation of the present moment, and gratitude. Today's activity is about mindfulness meditation. Read the instructions for this activity first.

Find a quiet place where you will be undisturbed. Sit with your spine straight and eyes closed. Start out by taking slow and deep breaths. Focus on your breath, how it feels as it enters your nose, throat, and lungs and then how it feels as it leaves your body. Notice, while paying attention to your breath, if you feel tension or pain anywhere in your body. Don't try to analyze it, just take a mental note and focus on breathing again. If thoughts or emotions pop up, let them pass as if they are scenes on a movie screen. If you catch yourself getting distracted, continue to bring yourself back to your breath. Do this for 15 minutes.

After the session, write about what you experienced.

_____

_____

_____

_____

_____

_____

_____

_____

_____

_____

_____

_____

_____

_____

Our busy minds create much of the stress we experience on a daily basis. When we identify with thoughts and emotions, we give them power. Many of us are also spending so much of our lives "doing" and thinking and not just "being." The key is to take the time to slow down and discover that the busyness of the mind exists but that it is not who we are. We truly are strong and peaceful at heart.

This mindfulness meditation technique is also great way to relieve stress. The more you practice it, the easier it becomes to be free of the mind's distractions. It helps bring clarity and peace—and sometimes even the solutions to certain things you may need in that moment. Try it a few times per week and remember that this inner peace is accessible at all times.

DAILY LOG: Day 10

NUTRITION LOG

Today I ate

Breakfast _____

Lunch _____

Dinner _____

Snacks _____

Drinks _____

Total calories consumed _____

Cravings _____

Total amount of water consumed _____

SLEEP LOG

Yesterday I slept _____ hours.

ACTIVITY LOG

Today I took _____ steps.

Types of physical activities performed _____

_____

_____

_____

_____

STRESS RELEASE LOG

Today I released stress by _____

_____

_____

_____

_____

GRATITUDE LOG

Today I am grateful for _____

_____

_____

_____

_____

MISCELLANEOUS REFLECTION

_____

_____

_____

_____

_____

_____

_____

_____

_____

Today give someone you love a hug
(this includes you).

Day 11:
Emotions

Affirmation

*I allow myself to experience and honor all of my
emotions in a healthy way.*

1. What range of emotions do you express regularly? Happiness,
   anger, depression?

_____

_____

_____

_____

_____

_____

_____

_____

_____

2. What range of emotions would you like to experience more?

_____

_____

_____

_____

_____

_____

_____

3. How do you cope emotionally with stressful situations? Do you withdraw, yell, or cry?

_____

_____

_____

_____

_____

_____

_____

Emotional well-being is just as important as physical well-being. In fact, everyone's core essence is happiness, peace, love, light, and all other feelings of positivity. We inherently know this exists, and this is why we are always trying to find peace. Many of us, however, look for this peace and happiness outside of ourselves but are never truly satisfied.

Emotions other than peace are signals that something is off. For example, feeling irritable may be a sign that our body is hungry or needs rest. Also, emotions are often triggered by certain negative thoughts or beliefs, many of which we have carried from our past. Take, for example, the emotion of fear, though not fear as it relates to survival (being afraid to jump out of an airplane actually serves us well). We may want to go forward with a goal in our lives but may be scared of failure. This fear of failure may have been instilled in us because our caregivers had this fear, or we may have had an experience in our past that we perceived as a failure. This fear from our past may continue to hold us back in our present and future. This is where mindfulness is so effective. Instead of reflexively reacting to our thoughts and emotions, we can stop and watch them and see where they are coming from, see that they are just thoughts and emotions, not who we are at our core.

Unfortunately, many of us have grown up believing that expressing our emotions is inconvenient or a sign of weakness and instead either hold in our emotions or deal with them in unhealthy ways. Since we often associate negative feelings with when these emotions arise, we may try to resist feeling the feelings. E-motions, however, are "energy in motion." When we do not express our emotions in healthy ways, negative energy builds inside our bodies, which can cause fatigue and stress and can lead to depression, infection, and other diseases. A lot of this unexpressed emotion is pain and hurt we still carry from our past and often try to mask with alcohol, food, or working too much.

Remember, the only way out, however, is through!

The key is to honor, feel, and release every emotion as it arises. Any time you feel a negative emotion or think a negative thought, don't resist it or judge it. Allow yourself to feel the emotion and, if needed, to express it in a healthy way. Watch the thought pass. Then take a breath and feel the emotion or thought float away.

DAILY LOG: Day 11

NUTRITION LOG

Today I ate

Breakfast _____

Lunch _____

Dinner _____

Snacks _____

Drinks _____

Total calories consumed _____

Cravings _____

Total amount of water consumed _____

SLEEP LOG

Yesterday I slept _____ hours.

ACTIVITY LOG

Today I took _____ steps.

Types of physical activities performed _____

_____

_____

_____

_____

STRESS RELEASE LOG

Today I released stress by _____

_____

_____

_____

_____

GRATITUDE LOG

Today I am grateful for _____

_____

_____

_____

_____

MISCELLANEOUS REFLECTION

_____

_____

_____

_____

_____

_____

_____

_____

Today take some time to allow yourself to feel and release emotions you have been holding in. You can do this by sitting and allowing them to come up and then letting them go.

Day 12:
Health

Affirmation

I am healthy and treat my body with respect.

1. What does the word health mean to you?

_____

_____

_____

_____

_____

_____

2. What are some unhealthy habits that prevent you from achieving optimal health?

_____

_____

_____

_____

_____

_____

_____

3. Many people smoke tobacco, drink alcohol, overeat, and use other unhealthy behaviors to self-soothe feelings of anxiety or sadness. Does this apply to you in any way? If so, from where do these feelings come?

_____

_____

_____

_____

_____

_____

4. Reflect on why you continue these habits, despite knowing the harm they cause your body. From where does the lack of self-appreciation come?

_____

_____

_____

_____

_____

_____

_____

_____

It is important to be aware of unhealthy habits and the need for them. In addition, being mindful of uneasy emotions, such as anxiety and depression, is key so that you can replace unhealthy coping techniques with healthy ones, such as breathing techniques or exercise. It's important to note, however, that sometimes we may use healthy habits such as exercise as unhealthy coping mechanisms to escape our feelings as well. While replacing an unhealthy distraction with a healthy one is better than doing nothing, the underlying issue still exists. Remember to be mindful of this impulse.

Our bodies are always sending us messages, and slowing down to feel our bodily sensations tells us a lot. You may have noticed during practicing mindfulness meditation that you hold tension in certain areas of your body. Some of us may feel symptoms without having to meditate, but many of us hold unease in our bodies without realizing it. For example, shoulder or neck pain may be a sign that we are carrying too much on our shoulders in terms of our responsibilities in life. Abdominal pain may be a sign that we are not eating healthy foods or that we are not dealing with stress appropriately. What do you think your body is trying to tell you?

DAILY LOG: Day 12

NUTRITION LOG

Today I ate

Breakfast _____

Lunch _____

Dinner _____

Snacks _____

Drinks _____

Total calories consumed _____

Cravings _____

Total amount of water consumed _____

SLEEP LOG

Yesterday I slept _____ hours.

ACTIVITY LOG

Today I took _____ steps.

Types of physical activities performed _____

_____

_____

_____

_____

STRESS RELEASE LOG

Today I released stress by _____

_____

_____

_____

_____

GRATITUDE LOG

Today I am grateful for _____

_____

_____

_____

_____

MISCELLANEOUS REFLECTION

_____

_____

_____

_____

_____

_____

_____

_____

Today practice patience.

If at any time you feel impatient,
take a moment to think about how
negative emotions or impatience will solve the situation.
They probably won't, so relax, breathe,
and enjoy being alive.

Day 13:
Gratitude

Affirmation

I am grateful for everything life has to offer me.

1. So far, throughout this journal, you've been asked to record things for which you are grateful. How often do you focus on your blessings instead of your problems?

_____

_____

_____

_____

_____

_____

_____

_____

_____

2. If you died tomorrow, what would your problems mean to you
   then?

_____

_____

_____

_____

_____

_____

_____

_____

_____

_____

For the rest of the day, if you catch yourself thinking of something bothering you, consciously replace the thought with something for which you are grateful. Remember, you most likely have the ability to read, money for basic necessities, a home, etc. Many in the world are not as fortunate. You could die tomorrow, but you are breathing and living right *now*. Life is a gift to be appreciated at every moment.

DAILY LOG: Day 13

NUTRITION LOG

Today I ate

Breakfast _____

Lunch _____

Dinner _____

Snacks _____

Drinks _____

Total calories consumed _____

Cravings _____

Total amount of water consumed _____

SLEEP LOG

Yesterday I slept _____ hours.

ACTIVITY LOG

Today I took _____ steps.

Types of physical activities performed _____

_____

_____

_____

_____

STRESS RELEASE LOG

Today I released stress by _____

_____

_____

_____

_____

GRATITUDE LOG

Today I am grateful for _____

_____

_____

_____

_____

MISCELLANEOUS REFLECTION

_____

_____

_____

_____

_____

_____

_____

_____

Today come up with your own positive theme for the day.

Day 14:
Present Moment

Activity:

Take thirty minutes to sit somewhere in nature where you will be undisturbed. Pay attention to everything around you—from the animals and trees to the colors, smells, and the way the air feels. Really appreciate every detail. If any thoughts or feelings arise, let them pass and focus your attention back on what is around you.

1. Reflect on your experience. How did you feel? Did you learn anything?

_____

_____

_____

_____

_____

_____

2. Record some events and situations from your past that bother you today.

_____

_____

_____

_____

_____

_____

_____

3. Note some events and situations you are worried about happening.

_____

_____

_____

_____

_____

_____

_____

4. At this very moment in time, what is happening in your immediate surroundings?

_____

_____

_____

_____

_____

_____

_____

5. Does anything from two or three have any bearing on what's happening in this moment?

_____ (By the way, the answer is *no.*)

Our problems from the past and our worries about the future have no bearing on what is going on right *now*, in this moment. We often waste the present moment with negative emotions, when we could instead be present and appreciate it. We spend so much time dwelling on the past that we get depressed and so much time worrying about the future that we become anxious—and so life passes us by. We look back and regret that we didn't enjoy the present moment, which was all that we had at that time, and then repeat the cycle. It's just a habit and we can change habits. It takes practice. Being present is what mindfulness and meditation is all about. For the rest of the day, be present. If at any time you feel tension or negative feelings, bring yourself back to what is going on in that exact moment.

DAILY LOG: Day 14

NUTRITION LOG

Today I ate

Breakfast _____

Lunch _____

Dinner _____

Snacks _____

Drinks _____

Total calories consumed _____

Cravings _____

Total amount of water consumed _____

SLEEP LOG

Yesterday I slept _____ hours.

ACTIVITY LOG

Today I took _____ steps.

Types of physical activities performed _____

_____

_____

_____

_____

STRESS RELEASE LOG

Today I released stress by _____

_____

_____

_____

_____

GRATITUDE LOG

Today I am grateful for _____

_____

_____

_____

_____

MISCELLANEOUS REFLECTION

_____

_____

_____

_____

_____

_____

_____

_____

_____

A New Beginning

I hope that over the past two weeks you were able to discover more about yourself. Please take time to reflect on the entire experience, involving both the activities and daily log. Were there things about yourself that you did not know before and know now? Is there anything you'd like to work on? Would you benefit from changing any habits related to your health?

_____

_____

_____

_____

_____

_____

_____

_____

_____

_____

_____

_____

A Note From the Author

Throughout the past fourteen days, you may have discovered certain issues you would benefit from working on, and this is OK. As discussed, bringing thoughts and emotions to light enables us to change for the better. If necessary, it may be well worth consulting with a physician or a counselor for further guidance. Healers are here to help us in times of need.

We all have within us the answers to our life questions. It's just a matter of asking and letting ourselves find them. This requires us to clear the busyness of our minds and buried emotions in our hearts that block the divine wisdom within. Mindfulness, meditation, presentness: these strategies allow the richness of life that exists within to flow. When you get to the point that you can look at life around you and feel content, it's a good sign that you have released the obstructions that have prevented your Light from shining.

I know this from personal experience. From the outside looking in, anyone would think I "had it all." Despite my achievements as a physician, I felt as if something was missing. I struggled with maintaining a healthy weight, and days on end passed when I did not want to get out of bed in the mornings. I remember on birthdays thinking, *Well I guess it's just another year I have to get through*. Life brought me, however, the circumstances I needed to wake up. I realized I was avoiding myself and had a lot of pain from my past of which I needed to let go. I didn't appreciate myself or know my true worth. With just a shift in perspective and attitude and a little letting go, I transformed my life completely for the better. You too are deserving and capable of having the life you desire.

One final note: nothing needs to be "fixed." Everyone is perfect because of his or her imperfections. Everything we go through in life is meant to direct us on a path to realizing our true self, a Divine being meant to express our Infinite nature.

Always remember to
just breathe and let go.

Made in the USA
Charleston, SC
21 November 2014